Three Birds Deep

Three Birds Deep

Poems by

Sheila Carter-Jones

Lotus Press
Detroit

International Standard Book Number:
978-0-9797509-5-3
0-9797509-5-4

Library of Congress Control Number: 2011942378

Printed and manufactured in the United States of America

Lotus Press, Inc.
"Flower of a New Nile"
18080 Santa Barbara Drive
Post Office Box Number 21607
Detroit, Michigan 48221

www.lotuspress.org

Acknowledgments

Grateful acknowledgment is made to the following publications in which some of these poems first appeared: *The Pennsylvania Review* ("How Far Down"); *Publish Today* ("8:30 a.m. Pittsburgh Color Line," "Here. Now. Nam.," "Circus Acts," "Ballerina," "Onyx Moon," "Mathematics of Tarot," and "Mad Dog Wind"); and *Madwomen in the Attic* ("Blue," "This Blue," "Urban Myth," and "Hydra-Boy").

I would like to express my appreciation to Jan Beatty, Ellen Smith, and Stacey Waite of Madwomen in the Attic workshops for their helpful comments and constant support and encouragement and to Toi Derricotte and Cornelius Eady for founding Cave Canem, a home for African American writers. I would also like to thank Juliette Hill who helped in shaping the manuscript. Most significantly, I wish to thank my husband, Bruce Jones, the man who matters most and who has cheered me on day after day without fail.

S.C-J.

Contents

I.

Save Me, Snake Charmer

Starry Night As Eden Snake

I am drunk on poppy seed, desert blue peyote
and I ride my blue zebra with rattle-
snake eyes that stare into a *Starry*
Night Over the Rhone.

Only in my dream do I know
this blue, white striped Z
is a horse with chestnut skin, the color
of my dining room buffet.

La Nuit Étoilée is a blue bicep that muscles
concentric stars through blue-brick night;
lays light in spasms of patterns that shiver
as a near dead flock of blue hues
that belly crawl to shore.

Only in my dream do I know
the blue boobed B is a brothel bitch
who guards carefully a left
ear lobe wrapped in newspaper
without detail about how the war
must go on, how Diane's two hands
learned to knit to make something to hold
now that her son is dead.

I paddle the boat of this post impression trip,
glimpse bold blue before taste of turpentine

turns me crystal soothsayer who yanks oars
of brain lesions as caught carp thrash from the lip.

Only in my dream do I know
this hiss-blue S is an Eden snake
with two blue tongues;
one explains the blue dreams,
one explains the blue dreams.

8:30 a.m. Pittsburgh Color Line

Saturday morning I see the neighbor kid John
waiting for the 7D-Perrysville Avenue bus.
I yell that I'm driving to the wholesale district;
he jumps in, pulls headphones from ears
to his lap. The rap flows on its own, makes
a static boundary that separates haves
from the half-knots woven between shared,
peculiar history.

We're about to cross the 16th Street Bridge
when we see green ketchup pouring down
a billboard advertised as new blood of America—
Heinz 57 American dream guaranteed to revive
sense of duty to hotdogs and apple pie.

Beneath that sweet green dream, new true blue
Ore Ida fries are lined like soldiers side by side.
I say to John, *The world is coming to color at last
and it's a good thing we are people of color.*
John says, *All we need now is some Soul Ketchup.*

What color would that be? I ask.
He says, *Black and blue like bruises.*
I tell him I too know the pain of color
and sometimes you don't know the hurt
is there until you see the mark on your skin,
like the Tallahatchie River full of Emmett Till's
true blue blood staining Mississippi's landscape.

Three Birds Deep

I

Mornings are hard for my father.
Three swallows of black coffee.
Tart flock down the throat
scrapes wings over grit of Republic
Steel Coal Mines.

The taste of black dirt is wafer
thin offering on tongues of demons
that heave in his chest,
cut words at three-quarters, hack
brutal dark as doctors carve
a first bird from the left lung:
a promiscuous street woman
nursing plumes the color of warm
strewn with shards of magenta.

II

Another bird, unexpected, found dead—
yellow canary, eyes filled with bits
wicked as tobacco born hungry for pull
of malignant winds that swell billows
in wings. An inhale barely expands
my father's chest. His raisin-brown skin
stretched to capacity of breath is no wind
storm brazen as the second hussy
hurled from black muck.

III

A third bird on twisted flutter
zips fast into my father's face,
pecks his dry mouth with razor beak.
Its ragged feathers scratch down in the throat
near a fourth bird hidden deep in criss-
cross branches of the right lung.

It sings that it will build a nest when earth
turns. Six months later, no nest to block
December shiver, and my father, without
bargain, gives last bits of air, helps the bird
bring sticks and twigs, make a home burrowed
out of reach, nestled in boughs of flesh.

My father roosts with old passerine crow
master of carcinogen wings, swaps stories
of flight, and in his mind of feathers
my father circle glides—lifts in transition,
kamikazes out of sight.

Here. Now. Nam.

I have seen some great change
but none as grand as the one
I watch my brother do. He can
cartwheel his mind back to the war,
then flip back into this moment—
just as quick, backward somersault
into that machete jungle full
of baby heads and infant guts.
And here, now, reclined on corduroy
Lazy-Boy, his own guts infected
with Mekong River blood, full
of H-I-Vietnamese carry out disease.

He hears gibber-jabber of enemy;
syllables slide and crouch low.
Now suddenly drunk and reeling
in some Saigon bar he sees
a slant-eye girl-child who speaks
what English she knows.
You want dope, Charlie?
I got good dope, Charlie.

Now in and out of the hospital
for veterans, my brother passes
red piss blood for urine sample,
nurses a belly swollen with Viet
Nam War water waist high
same as he waded, gun overhead
each arm stretched up, pinned

against heaven, AK-47 crucified.
Said he prayed, *Take all of me here now,*
Nam. I can't roll a stone in three days.

Yesterday I asked him,
How's your liver?
and this is what he sang:
> *My liver! My liver!*
> *I spit it out.*
> *They gave me a new one.*
> *I swallowed it whole and*
> *it wiggled right into place.*
> *Now I'm doing just fine.*

Circus Acts

Someone painted a wiggly line
down the side of my white car,
a snake I discovered in black grass
of Sunday morning when hallelujah freaks
roam earth as drunk soldiers. And how
unusual the anger that didn't rise in me
as the bible says, Jesus got up from the dead
after three days; scared everybody
to death until they called him Savior.

Save me, snake charmer, before I cry,
Liar on the high wire!

I can paint worse sins than that neophyte
Eve ever dreamed in used-to-be Eden,
where apples turned red temptation
like Queen of Hearts' caricature breasts
caressed by cheating fingers
at the edge of a throw-away pile,
red diamonds dull, clubbed feet scratching
in a game of rummy, sequins, whiskey breath.

Save me, snake charmer, before I cry,
Cheater in the Garden—Gin!

Boxes, apple crates, pineapples and piña
coladas float in water just beyond port,
baptized by longshoremen who grant
entry into marketplace beyond Golden Gates,

where people know so much sin they hiss
a prayer for every lie they ever told
about heaven: strutting through pearly gates
to hang with Gabriel and other flying freaks
who fold fashion wings over new virginity,
let frayed grips of chastity belts
drop to earth gently worn.

Save me, snake charmer, before I scream,
Grab one smelly trinket for me!

Two Men: On Women

Black widow. Ever see one?
They have that red octagon.

I see them every day downtown.
Those motherfuckers will eat you alive.

From the inside out they'll eat you,
leave the shell.

The female eats the male.

Same as the praying mantis.

Blue

I go back to pull blue
between oak tree
leaves spread wide,
to grasp blue in a sky
I stood under.

That day I never felt
the shale slide,
my feet slip,
catch together.
I just got tangled
in all the blue swirls
that stretched
endless blue.

Silent and still
blue as that day
hung upside down;
a paisley blue bluefish
slipping through fingers,
rushing wild for blue.

Blue, I never heard
my feet slip and catch
on sliding shale that day
I swallowed the sky.
I never heard myself fall up
swept in tumbles, begging
blue-lipped into mighty blue.

Blue, I didn't know
I was shaking, breaking apart;
never anticipated the dismembering,
cruel pull of blue
separating each
piece of me falling
deep into blue.

Call it all the way
to China blue.

Call it so blue
that I suffocate
in its comforting arms.

II.

Blue Comet of Blueberries Streaks in Me

This Blue

This is the blue I have been getting to, the blue-
berry blue of early summer that melts
down the finger, sticks. That's the way
I remember the thick finger of a left hand
fox-nosed into thickets of shaded blue blankets.
A right hand held its weight a blue breath inch
from my brown-blue body; that's when I saw the ice-
angel float away to another blue world, unsweetened—
out of reach of sailboats with lungs full of blue that blow
from the bedspread a blue iris on chenille waves
ten thousand miles high, blue.

I felt the clump split and I knew
blue would splash, knew that I could not stop
blue burst of feathers, could not stop
the wont of blue to fly away. Bluebird
down my throat, circle me in its season of color,
cradle me in a nest of blue. Not like this forced blue
that made me crave flight too soon—before chasing
blue light of fireflies, before leg-blue scratch of crickets
and before the numbing chill of submissive blue,
the feel-good blue of supple tissue rubbed raw.

The blue comet of blueberries streaks in me still,
even after billions of blue Sundays in heaven's blue
box of prayer and redemption. I nurse blue shame
in intricate folds of the labia, like lacerated flesh
covered with thin blue skin, my negligee tangled
in secret vines too drenched in blue to recognize,

17

need of blue to release and flow over dried
layers of vulva that have long been
two sunken ships abandoned in vicarious blue.

Urban Myth: Man-Man

Daddy longlegs crawled up the backside
of a porcelain tub, stretched its legs
in all ten directions like Swamp Man's fingers
spread wide. He reached
two hands, snatched shoulders, sucked
me down whole into quicksand of his lap, fast,
unyielding as slippery slope of porcelain
under Harvestman's long leg daddy knees
bent in stiff concentration.

What to do? How to move?

I sit chiseled on Swamp Man's flesh-
chair; the back rises,
crazy rhino lost in the sand;
head pokes my spine with one
crust of horn, forces.

What to do? How to move?

Big Daddy L.L.
takes his time, measures
possibility of motion needed
to balance weight /no-weight.
What to do—
how to move without losing rhythm of eight
legs in concert, tumbling headlong
down the spiraling song of the drain.

I get caught up in the headmeat
of Swamp Man's words that spin inside my belly;
feel gritty horn of rhino jerk,
wild and mean. It slip-slides
as bog-talk drowns.
Big Man in the city says,
I'm gonna tame you.

What to do—how to move—how to
push thick weight of two legs away
from wide open mouth—all talk,
no bite.

Elegy for Douglas Mason
(May 31, 1945-January 20, 2010)

When at last January's song was sung,
there at bedside I held his hand, squeezed a melody.
I did all but sing the words out loud, my lips
two petals quivering purple in the dawn.

And a hand on the head patted him *So long*,
as he skipped across the boney dump to sit
by the creek where awaited his fishing rod,
one long branch from the neighbor's willow tree
weeping slender leaf tears for Doug, my brother dear.

And way up in the gray cloud sky I could hear
a crow's caw bury sorrow in the snow
as mid morning sun climbed a dirge of steel gray,
lit the way for ruddy red-brown man with boyish face
who had all but expired. At beside I promised
green in early spring when lush along the pipeline grew
blackberries and plums whose sugars crusted over summer,
fermented homemade wine when October frost was done.

I asked no questions as the cold moved in.
Baby birds played all day and cried at dark,
their chilly feathers tucked inside the nest
when death came calling using our mother's breath.
Calling for you, my brother dear, to come home
from playing between tunnels in piles of cinder rock,
take the dirt path, push tamarack and tall weeds back.

I knew it was you there at the edge of cinder and woods,
your eyes shaded with that famous southpaw, shoulders
leaned left as you walked along tracks until the train
roared beyond the trestle, its whistle distant in the hollow
where wild violets grow in poultice of coal ash pyre—
bit of dust enough, brother dear, to take your breath away.

Eaves Dropping

It is the homely neighbor's fist banging
that brings me quickly walking, almost
trotting to the door. It is Charlotte,
out of breath, hair a gray-brown matted nest
this September morning,

arms uncontrollable branches
bent by eighty-five years of wind.
Out of sorts she is; bats at thoughts
rising from her head crazed as crows
that crash with ebony beaks and pull fast
bits of road kill guts.

Charlotte babbles breathless as child with wings
who flies home to tell. Her hand grabs fistful
of hair, pulls in morning light.
Each strand, a crusted curl of confusion,
soars, swoops down, alights then up
to quick flight. Too many thoughts rise,
fall before glide, and gathering herself
she says, *I don't mean to bother you, but*
there's a eagle under your front porch eaves.
You know you got a nest up 'ere.

I tell Charlotte that eagles are rare in these parts—
in fact, endangered by no fault of their own
but by humans, who hunt other humans
in wars, disputes and spats, and in love.

It's always beak to mouth, sharing of tongue
that joins, feeds, separates in ruin.

This is when Charlotte changes her story.
Well, maybe it's a cat.
I ask, *Why would a cat be sitting in a nest?*
Charlotte changes the story again:
Oh, it's probably a squirrel, then. Yeah, a squirrel.
A squirrel could get up that high. Couldn't it?
Now Charlotte has rendered me fuzzy-tailed;
no words, confounded by muddled morning mist
that has brought her beneath the eaves pointing now.
See! See! It's somethin' up 'ere.

The Housing Authority: On Mice and Men

Fuck it. They have to live too.

They're not going to bother you.

They come with the house.

I wondered when they were going to show up.

Pretty Boy

My brother said,

I seen more dead people than the average undertaker—
rows of bodies like meat on slabs.
The rice was good over there though,
not like here.

And serving up rice grain memory from over there, he said,

It was the worst thing I ever seen.
Over there that air conditioned tent
was a makeshift refrigerator,
a freezer to keep bodies from cooking
in that Nam heat.

I was in there once when they called me to identify my buddy.
When they unzipped the bag
I was glad he had his head.
Some of those guys didn't even
have their heads no more,
but Chas had his and he
had his arms and he had
his legs— and everything.

I couldn't tell if he was really dead or playing around.
But it wasn't funny when I seen
shrapnel sticking out the back
side of his head. Other than that,
it wasn't a mark on him.

He still had a head full of curly hair, pretty-boy, dark Italian hair.
That's what we called him,
Pretty Boy.

Ballerina

Flowers plié,
birds arabesque
the moon, Diana
streaming love talk
through night's dark moves.

Currents run
lazy and satisfied
into new day breaking;
drops of dew,
fading passions,
fields of gray mist
accent sun's blurred vision.

On the back porch
a jar with chipped mouth
dares not speak words
that may disturb
silence of me
leaving your bed
on ballerina toe-tips.

Sky Like This

2 p.m. December 11th I hear swoosh
of air pushed through Carolyn's vocal chords,
forced to form the *ugh* sound that moves
through the throat, a fish out of water
that cannot come to full gulp.
The word *again,* caught.

In that breath Carolyn tells me nurses
and doctors will collect money, give it
to her. She says, *I never had any money*
come out of a sky like this. I can only
be grateful for a gift out of the clear blue.

We talk about how she is reinventing
herself with fewer pounds. She says,
I don't know who I am. But at fifty-six
I must be somebody.
I guess you could say I'm like a shooting star.
Everything piled up on me, got so heavy
I just had to come down.

Down to a size eight after having always wanted
to be a cute little arrangement of cheeks and bones.
People mention she is thin and she tells them,
It is a recent thing, but does not say what
the *thing* is. She just says, *The time for skinny*
is here, but she wants her fat back,
all two-hundred forty-seven pounds.

The One Winged Moth

I.
Near the door I found it. Scratch of message:
one winged moth lying in unspoken words,
heaviness between two lovers
who break apart, feel the full weight
of a single body that cannot lift
itself into flight.

Drag of abdomen against grist of cement
gives it beauty, the force of will
to bring itself to full flutter, and I confess
I want to learn how small creatures pull,
break from attachment,
move on.

It is not so much to ask: just to know
that after things have gone so wrong
one can crawl haltingly away
from that counted as necessary, live
close to what is uncompromising
in its fullness.

It is true; this is what my mother called
a beautiful woman, and knowing this
makes me want to hold my lover's head
hard to my breast until the mouth
breaks flesh, pours altitude into me.

II.

The one winged moth as something of beauty
is truth I am not certain of— dragging movements
too close to how I have learned to hide hurt,
cocooned in mid-air preparation to reinvent
myself in the blind dark of pupae chrysalis.

Hidden like my mother buried in years,
waiting in blue-black thick of day, wandering
rooms as blood pulses beneath skin thin enough
to see empty chambers of a structure precisely placed—
meant to be private.

This is what she did not know she wanted: for me
to stand in shadows, pretentious as gestures
that welcome dark like morning before night lifts,
before larval skin splits me awake and wings
tear through the obscure.

III.

Stiff in the Dead-Dream

One Act Poem: Son/ New Native

Background:
Mr. Word Smith is seen locking
his front door with special key
that locks his hair in dreads. Walks
to corner, stands. Cups mouth with hands.
(Loudly)
This poem is a metaphor for a blink,
a spark, a flinch, a sniff—born dead
a flicker, drop, taste, pittance—public
housing community— the projects/a plan
not the kind you see in the suburbs.

This poem is not a staged reality scene
where some director (if there is one)
shouts, *Okay, everybody start fucking,*
shooting, smoking crack, etc., etc.
It is 9:11 P.M. Ghost dark.
Eastern Standard Time. America.
(Mr. Word Smith up and leaves.)

Scene One:
A Black Boy runs from Ms. Millie's back door.
A Blue Man talks into his shoulder
device rigged for sound.

Scurry of feet, flurry of bullets, scatter
of brains on pavement. Blue Man is riddled,

excitement twisted on his tongue, (shouts)
Black is suspect, black down, boy down
black suspect is boy. Black boy down.

Not a call for back-up. It is an announcement,
(cries out) *We got another one.*
Sheer joy of chase, hunt is what Blue
People relish as dog slaps tongue
around snout after good taste of steak, sits,
waits, a good doggy for the next Black Boy.

No need for ambulance to hurry; no need
for siren to part sea of spectators; no need
to drown tears of emergency. Black Boy
pronounced dead, absorbed in concrete.

Scene Two:
The neighborhood poet, Mr. Word Smith, re-enters.
(Smoothly, angrily) *Black Boy*
should have slipped into his panther body
as he ran—should have become like Bearden,
brushed night across canvas of the projects,
stroked so wide— is no difference
between black and night.
Black Boy should have . . . . (Voice fades)

> (Cut to Black Boy's mama crying on sidewalk,
> Word Smith's voice a seamless layer
> glazed between muffles.
> Low moans, mumbles rise from crowd
> burn with city heat.)

Same ol', same ol'.
Black on black crime.
Do it, pay with life.

(Zoom in)
Black Boy's mama is a red T-shirt,
nylon sweats; two white tracks run down legs
where her fifteen-year-old baby lies dead.
Mama's body shakes. She is not an eruption
spewing black female fire, mouthful
of motherfuckers. She is a volcano of tears.
Colliding blackbird hands flit to find place to perch,
a jagged edge that does not burn with hurt.

Young-bow-tie reporter shoves through crowd,
pushes mic to Black Boy's mama's lips.
She screams guttural moan. (Reporter pulls mic back to self;
pushes, eager for details.)
What happened here? (wiggling mic as he
ejaculates fast stream of questions.)
Is it true Black Boy was breaking, entering?
Is it true Black Boy had a gun, a magnum?
Is it true Black Boy fired at Blue Man?

(Black Boy's mama, head in hands, gulps air
catches breath, shock-talks.)
I don't
know what
happened.
They called
 me— said

my son
was down—
fuckin' shot.
That's all
the fuck
I heard.

Curtain.

Onyx Moon

In the bloodshot eyes of my father
I see the moon roll red with fever,

hot like those summer nights when darkness
was a crazed crow flitting through blackness,

its plumage pressed against the body—
wingless as Nippy, John and Ollie

who worked swing shift on Saturday nights,
picked and heaved curse words as religious rites,

breathed black of bituminous chunks
that fell as onyx stones into load car dust

and the brakeman rode the cap-piece cockeyed-drunk,
yelling, *Watch out for crows, 'cause ain't no train track*

leading straight to no onyx moon.

How Far Down

The whistle from the coal mines
still burns in my ears and I swear
I hear feet trudging the path:
muffled morning voices of men
moving into darkness below.

How far down do coal miners go?

How far down before their faces
are voices in dust, their laughter
burning chunks in the throat?
How far down before eyes
are sapphire sparks, breath
smoldering cinders?

How far down do coal miners go
before their bones burn to white ash,
tongues turn bituminous black?
I just want to know.

How far down do they go?
How far down?

Bee Keeper

alone with three legs reaching,
a yellow jacket lay like a virgin in the grave
curled on cool basement cement,
stiff in the dead-dream.

it would have been easy
to kick it away, toe to head—how it should be
if it had not awakened
my brother in me.

he crouched, still at war,
wounded flesh unhealed from elbow to phalanges.
His writing hand cupped blood—
southpaw, unlucky in love.

how did this soldier bee
fly down rice-paddy laundry chute into knick-knacks, hunks
of chairs piled one
on top of two, three and twenty-five

hexagonal cells? Reconfigured,
this mass of wood is a bone hive of mangled bodies
thrown in a stack
of unidentified honeycombs.

trees full of slant eye chom-chom
grow their white Viet-meat transparent as wafer wings
my brother used
when he flew into me—sideways.

the body he left behind
is full of thick skin for ceremony to ashes;
this gray-brown dust
I keep on the tongue stings my eyes.

Business of Black

When I ask if she is the only African
American in the program, she is two
quick hands that shake ten fingers fanned
wide before my eyes. She corrects, *No . . .*
No, I am from the Bahamas. Her two eyes
dart behind spread of loose twigs
as if flutter of blackbird can wake me
from this black blunder. My tongue
wrestles in repeat like wings caught
in thicket of teeth and jaw. I almost say
Bohemian instead of Bahamian; just
get it in my head before zigzag synapses
strike a disconnect.

This thing called blackness hangs between,
grown from roots of cane plants, has lasted
many cycles before worn thin as warp/weft
time stretched beyond us in machete business
chopped here. Stalks of no leaves are no arms
wrapped around breasts, no hands to rub
sugar juice on lips smooch-suckled
to mamma nipples that sing silent lullaby.

What burns now in this space where I breathe
charred memory of plantation cane?
And don't I hear her faint voice say, *Hair*
is naturally curly? Not that I would call it
by any other curvature in history, though
styled 'fro might suffice; parted, towered

toward the up-side to separate kinks,
like this thin-skinned moment grips hands,
pinches with stained fingers, peels
our blackness back to reveal a place thick
with manufactured sweetness gritty as difference
between front and backside of the same thing,
not wanting to be like itself.

The Pseudo Linguist: On the English Language

The Oriental guy, he spoke perfect English,
must be American born.
His daughter
also Oriental, English
speaking . . . blah-blah-blah
and most are inherently racist.

The Handkerchief's Catharsis

Handkerchiefs are small little creatures
that live huddled in recesses of pockets and purses.
They take human hurt and sorrow as their design
and curl quietly into themselves.

My grandmother's handkerchief is enclosed in her hand
as she lies in silent sleep blanketed to waist in teal blue
coffin, the color of spring robin's egg and full
of baby bird liquid.

She dreams wings.

Crow's Feathers

Ten on the high side
of the arc, silver lamp
pole balances crows,
all black silhouettes
shadowed in early
gray mist of this
Pittsburgh morning.

One has turned
its head to nine
tails. Two button
eyes dart this
way and that.

In one split
second it
disappears,
flits in flurry
of tail feathers.

IV.

Until I Sing My Mumbo-Jumbo Song

Mathematics of Tarot

I.

I met a card reader back in '68,
purple shawl rolled velvet ocean
waves over her shoulders, red rose
pinned behind her ear. I knew
she would tell me everything,
give it to me straight like wooden slats
that lined the front porch, close but not
touching

II.

I was gray and in between black and night
when that lady pulled a plain white
napkin from freshly baked biscuits
like a magic trick, abracadabra. She held
up the offering as if it appeared from thin air.
Just one for the road, she teased as I pushed
buttery crumbs around my mouth.

III.

My tongue remembers this circle story
that occurs or does not occur now
in a time of empty space back in the '60s.
Still I taste the probability of words in the dark
when the neighbor's dog yelps, scratches its fleas.
I tell myself if I were younger I would pierce
my tongue, lust for hard push of cold spike
to rip layers of muscle as a hooked fish jerks,
thrashes in mid-air, pulls

to drive the puncture deep into rim of lip.
Reel me in, reel me in, pull.
I want to feel swell of blood down the throat
until I sing my mumbo-jumbo fish song.
Pull me in, pull me in, roll the reel and pull.

Can't you hear the catfish wailing in my belly?

Helmet Head

In the driveway a grasshopper hops the hood,
clings like an ornament while I ride the passenger seat
shotgun, wild woman throwing peyote dust,
turning my car into a cluster of white palomino
clomping to pow-wow in the high desert.

My father on the day of his funeral
changed into a white bird. A seagull.
He had never been to the edge, never too
far past sulfur brown in the creek, but I had
once seen what could have been a gull gliding
above the Allegheny River, out of place
in the gray over Pittsburgh.

It is the same coughed up sky I saw
when my father's red-brown skin stretched death-ash
after living in coal mines, shaping dirtscapes
for rich people— boulders, manure, bulbs' stinking
possibilities buried in hardened feces like cape castle
walls made of human excrement. Millions
of embedded hearts still pulse there

as mine does now as I lean, my body
half out the window, screaming a fist at the grasshopper.
It hugs the hood with all six feet, madman with helmet head
bent to the wind. Wings press against abdomen,

protect the singing heart inside segmented armor-shell.
No need to flick it for choice of song. Force of wind

will knock the helmet off as we gain speed;
it will tumble backward, splatter on the windshield,
become a dot.

P.T.S.D.

Post:
after shock
body quake
nerves shake
withdrawal.

Traumatic:
psychological wound
drama Cong Queen
grenade in Viet vagina
blows rice paddy scene.

Stress:
tension stretched
test level; distressed
zero tolerance
synapses snap.

Disorder:
confused sinew
mind warp/weft wobbly
brutal behavior.

War.

The Gutting

Pull this cat-
fish out of me.
It is eating my food
and my stomach
is hungry for love.

Get this fish out of me.
It's entangled in intestines,
squeezing the carp out of me.
Grab a whisker in each hand
and jerk its neck
if it has one.

Otherwise, cut
the head from fin and tail;
guide the primal blade
and sever it away
from pumping gills.

It would be torture
to let the cat-
fish flip flop until fatigue
forced finality. Pinch
the nose to stop it
from breathing in
its own pain.

Don't let those black
button eyes hypnotize,

the stuttering mouth
mesmerize with that
slow-O motion, silent wa-
wa-water pity talk.

Squeeze it down
with a choke-hold grip
before it slips back
to the creek. Make it
drown from too much air,
flip dead, gills up stiff
in the empty sink.

Hatch

At first I think it's a robin's egg fallen
too far from the nest, but it's a small rock
hard and unforgiving in its density;
like my mother's mind, a winding disc
stuck in a groove, calling my sister-in-law's
name. *Come here, Barbara,* she says, and by
that name I go to her, become flesh and blood
of coagulated memories crammed bumper-
to-bumper in thought jams.

I turn this rock around, feel smooth
lacerated lumps of tar worn against granite-shell;
see that not even this rock is exempt from scarred skin,
and its fleshy tones give possibility of a bird inside a shell
like my mother who will become beak and feathers,
fly from the gray matter. And suddenly,
a surge of oxygen in my brain makes me jerk,
afraid the rock will hatch in my hand too soon

and clear liquid will ooze without form, without
voice. I will touch the primordial slime,
cling to what my mother's bones will become,
take on her form. I will smell it. Take it in
on swell of lungs, wrap myself in fresh-born warmth,
fledgling breath; and instinct sure my mother
will accept her own beak, see with beady eyes
a way out of her shell of immense dark;
leave this nettle-nest world.

Mad Dog Wind

I keep hearing that mad dog wind howl through the valley,
scratch at windows of company store houses,
rattle bone chimes long empty of marrow.
It is the sound of my father's bedridden beg for air,
sanctified preacher's mouthful of prayer.

It must have been the way wind's cool wet hands
bent the screen door back until it creaked like lungs
pressed against forty years of December ice.

A boxcar full of storm-horses is headed this way;
some old hooded coal miner hangs on, arms
wrapped around one slick neck, hugs the rail
until air sacs are wrought with black disease.

It must have been the way the wind rattled the screen door
that makes me hear my father's breath—slow draw in
a steady release of pick and shovel life to machines
that lend steady push/pull of air into cavities
being eaten by the creeping dark of the coal mines.

Funny how it all begins to come back to me, what I didn't see:
his aluminum lunch pail empty on the shelf, gray work pants
folded away, boots with bituminous scars that say skin
over pain is never a pretty thing.

And funny, until now I never noticed my father
had grown old, not even when months before he asked

for a cane; didn't notice the knee of his right leg
could hardly bend up the back steps; just saw the smile
he worked his face so hard to make.

Social Worker: On the Homeless

Street life.
You know how the streets do you—
beat you up,
make you strange.

Paradise

The primordial vagina:
an exponential pleasure
mistaken for love,

the hyperbolic function
factors in per-
mutations of normal;

variables of possibility
is what could be
maybe right now.

No more privilege,
no more concern
for the dead

and dying stripes
that stand impenetrable
as gray granite

in the infinite
graveyard of men,
women and canine

who live within
boundaries of gray
interiors. This is all

I know of
us. We who
are metaphors of

place, the land
that owns identity,
claims, disclaims,
reclaims miniscule
damages done;

rank and file wear
dead soldiers tangled
around the neck
and dangled

against fiery throats
of those who love
complexities burning

on psychic landscapes.
Those who conquered
Paradise have designed

a new garden
full of crows
squawking and dancing
their pecking order.

V.

No Sound Pounds the Ear Drum

Where Some People Get Mixed Up
About the Meaning of Hello

I

Behind the counter of the mom and pop market on Brilliant
Avenue,
a woman, hair made of string, rings the cash register, starts a
rattle
up the throat. Broken baby-doll voice ekes out syllables, shutter
eyes
flip: *My mother gets as dark as you.*
Excited blush. She pushes blonde from her face, takes a breath;
I thrust my copper brown arm toward her—skinny legged model
prancing on runway, toes controlled, pointed sharp. I say,
You mean like this beautiful brown? in a voice that means
something
about the science of making dirt more nutritious.
(i.e. *Don't hand me that bullshit.*)

II

Geared up again, she recounts how her mother got stopped at the
border,
could not enter America coming home from vacation. Cancun
sun changed her.
The color of you, woman says. Passport photo clearly shows the
white woman smiling
was not this brown, cause for reasonable suspicion blocked at the
border.
That's funny, I say in a voice that means something
about living your whole life with lots of stops—halts.
(i.e. *Kiss my black consciousness.*)

67

III

Coming through customs nobody believed in her mother's skin,

woman explained, until strap of halter top was pulled back and
the fence

patrol could see that her mother was white underneath. Woman's
lips flutter.

Oh, by the way, you have gorgeous brown skin and blah, blah,
blah, blah, blah.

Keeps going as if her barbed wire voice is made to corral my
thoughts, silence me.

Really, I say in a voice that means,

This is not about your vagina on Broadway.

(i.e. *Shut the fuck up.*)

Hydra-Boy

I

Spin a curve on Perrysville Avenue,
see a small boy bundled, wearing
a blue tassel hat topped with white yarn ball.
In the early glare I wonder, What
kind of mother has pushed her small
child outside unsupervised to hold
with baby fingertips this 7A.M.
Pittsburgh morning, far too early
for play?

Who knows what child-eating monster
sloshes webbed feet around baby breath
of city bends, stalks just beyond
curved lip of concrete, a mouth
curled like Mama's arms, ready
to scoop and seduce the fast
legged avenue.

II

I pump the brake to slow my gaze—
almost yell, *Hey, kid! Where's your mama?*
but on close approach I see the small boy
has turned into a fire hydrant with a blue
bolt-head. I would run this iron
boy down, sure, for his ability
to corrode my perception,
threaten to explode.

I want to hunt down my father's monkey wrench,
the one with the barrel head,
its grooved teeth, uneven and unfair.
I want to clamp-grip the tassel head,
strip the small hat away, watch Hydra-Boy
drown in morning gray.

Revolution Reruns

Years after the fistful of revolution in the Sixties
I met Angela face to face; her 'fro
yet a prickly cactus shotgun steady
and full of protest. I was tight with her still
in the punch of clenched rights aimed straight
to disrupt the atmosphere.

Back then, there was no philosophy bending
blackness to mere theory of disorder, disturbance,
or dis-negro gone mad. We had purpose; articulate,
liberate, *Kill whitey.*

And the whitey concept was your mama telling you,
Stop all that crazy talk, like my mama told me
that summer night I left home. Eyes aflame with rage,
nose shooting death smoke, I was stoked
for change.

Hopped in Daddy's 1960 Chevy. Its back end heaved
sharp like coal miner's lungs as I drove straight
on the mark into city fire that choked with bare hands
until I came to my senses. From a bamboozled stupor
I stumbled

to consciousness. At the edge of the block I spotted
black hands brick black business glass, grab high-priced
TVs, and in pairs carry them home to watch reruns
of riots on KDKA News, shout,
Look! There I go. That was me, bro.

No Sound Pounds

No sound pounds the ear drum of those who sleep too late.
I talk and laugh and laugh-talk all night, like
young American, English Bowie and African Naomi,
do the daddy longlegs strut, knees pumped high. Then four
stiff legs fast-stomp down a heart-spike in the chest
that kills me dead as the day my mother decided to die.

No sound pounds the ear drum of those who sleep too late
like pre-babies born dead as chili beans in a tin can,
caught in thickness of sauce-blood, processed to last
nine months barring no interplanetary juxta-
movement when the moon flips into the eighth house.

No sound pounds the ear drum of those who sleep too late
like the no-babes of infertility who never come a-knocking
at the door of no-dreams. Neither do they phone home
with no sound that pounds down the door of those
who snore too loud in the dead-dream.

The Scholar: On Farming

I see pigs
every time somebody says,
I'd like to piggy-back
on that.

Helmet Head's Episode

I see it first thing:
a grasshopper stiff as twig in the produce section
so still it could be hand painted on collard leaves—
a blend of khaki skin on Hooker's green canvas,
camouflaged in war gear. Nearly invisible
in VERITAS verdant the six-legged soldier
is statued in silent psychotic dilemma.

I detect rattle of instinct in insect brain.
Hexagonal lenses take in leaf and stalk bunched,
tied like POWs marched to urban jungle
camp where green syllables slice thora-spine.
The segmented bodies tumble—fraught
with variations of vert.

I have tailspinned this way,
mandibles rigid, head dense in thoughts
overgrown with shrubs, hands clutched
to variegated possibilities, afraid to take the leap.

Grasshopper eyes scrutinize a Rorschach greengrocer
test, fixated to find familiar algorithms among
variables of greens, broccoli, politics and chive.
It senses light and dark, splat of green/splotch
of people; the calculations systematic,
locate by radar signal. I receive the S.O.S.
and I confess—I am linked by instinct to fear
 of finger pinch.

In tableaus of darker greens I have been unseen
against hues of market chaos, out of place among . . . . .
wearing herringbone skin fashioned over veins
fine as any membranous suit of wings.

I know what this field-hopper feels, the way foot soldiers
probe for landmines that scatter the brains. It understands
it dare not move in this space of shared food—waxy eco-helmet
no iron armor against marchand de legumes guarded
by grunt of human carnivore, prod of hands that force
ganglia-brain to hypothesize quickness of six legs leaping,
the faith of one helmet head catapulting to flight.

Die Laughing

My brother talks
with his trigger finger,
rapid fire words
laughing and crying
all at once.

Learned how
crouched in rice
paddies fertilized
with Vietnamese feces
(didn't matter whose
or what's).

He can AK-
47 you down
to your knees,
make you die
laughing, but not
back in Nam.
Said dying was
different— killed kids,
babies, mothers.

Said that was nothing
to laugh about
but he did, all night
smoking black tar

opium mixed with
oriental weed packed
in aluminum foil pipes.

Said he laughed
hardest when he
saw heads explode,
skull bone break, brains
fly, pieces of body
slap his face like he
had done something
wrong.

Said he
followed orders,
chain of command,
and if he hadn't
laughed so hard
he would have killed
himself.

Said war killing
was joke-time
until he came home,
both arms blacklined
like secret operations
inked on overlay maps
of Hotel Company,
2nd Battalion,
3rd Marine Regiment,
1st Platoon.

Death Squad—
first out
first hit.

Baby Leg

A woman comes rolling in her wheelchair,
elbows bent like chicken wings, hands
gripped on the wheels, and I bet
she flies in her dreams—
doesn't have to think about lifting
one leg in front of the left one
that is not there.

The right leg is a baby-leg,
new flesh with bare foot curled
just a little, as if caught
in some other space-time
and stayed there.

She spins spokes in straight line purpose,
appointment with free weights,
strength of upper body muscle.
She doesn't look at me even when
I say *Hello*. I don't know if she really
doesn't see me or doesn't want me
to see her baby-leg and the empty-space
leg that is not empty at all.

I imagine this woman into a world
Of a man I know who decided (only
he knows why), before becoming form,
before flesh, to enter a body with a left
arm like her right leg, short and paralytic,
of no use but to stir my thoughts.

She does not know (not yet
conscious of why) she, too, wanted this:
some of her life energy compressed
into one baby-leg with no growth cycle
and the other leg
a figment.

This unknowing presses her self-conscious
against me. My stomach pushes back.
Pressure of our masses insists in a space
of time kept as seed. I reach—know
I have a promise to keep, here, at this
moment of influence, but her woman-hand
is quick on the knob.

Zebra in the Graveyard

Zebra in the graveyard
leans on its front legs; hind
legs kick at finality of stone, and no-
body hears a word it says or sees
a silent tear roll down and stay—
just sees it statued there,
ass upturned to heaven
begging no forgiveness
for density of tomb.

The granite is hard as nails
hammered in a heart like the time
I was abandoned in modern hypocrisy—
sought balance in ancient science
that unlocks wisdom of body, of mind
and may come to the movie screen real
soon. For now I sit contorted, right leg
bent, pulled to breast, ankle pressed
against the left knee, crazy glued
in bone chime harmony.

I wish I could sing melodies
learned in the womb, complicated rhythms
of urban indecision; no rhyme-reason,
not like big Al's $E=mc2$ and not
like Isaac's up-must-come-down-to-dirt.
Like the Z, I'm all striped up, can't make up
my mind. Here I'm light, then dark, then dark

and light again, lost in art of people talk, con-
versational gibberish with words that dig
beneath skin.

Word-bombs aimed straight explode left
ventricle, shellshock absurdity as darkness
of that chamber sets in, and we are all
zebras carved in stone, asses high up in wind,
defying speed of light like life gone by too fast,
hightailed on an eight hour tour of Union Dale
Division No.3—cemetery where all tourists
just can't believe the stiff lipped Zed
soothsaid plain as day, *In the fourth world be
careful of snakes that fill mouths with pomegranate
in this retro/ E-garden. All penumbra beings
gathering countless seeds had better take heed of Z.*

The Senior Citizen: On Taking Medication

Sometimes
the side effects
are worse than what you got.

About the Author

Sheila L. Carter-Jones earned her Ph.D. in English Education from the University of Pittsburgh. An active member of the National Council of Teachers of English, she is also a teacher consultant for the Western Pennsylvania Writers Project at the University of Pittsburgh. She is one of the few but growing number of nationally board certified teachers in the school district where she taught for any years. Sheila has also taught various courses in the Education Department of several local colleges and universities. Included in her repertoire are numerous writing workshops which she developed to motivate and to act as scaffolds for novice and young writers.

She grew up in a small mining town in Western Pennsylvania and credits the domestic working women in that community as the spiritual source of her poetic inspiration. Much of her personal writing highlights the people and events in that small place where big dreams were nurtured.

Sheila is a fellow of Cave Canem and author of a chapbook, *Blackberry Cobbler Song*. Dr. Elizabeth Alexander served as judge of this year's Naomi Long Madgett Poetry Award and selected *Three Birds Deep* as the winner.